CW00395053

WARRIOR • 134

FRENCH *POILU* 1914–18

IAN SUMNER ILLUSTRATED BY GIUSEPPE RAVA

First published in Great Britain in 2009 by Osprey Publishing,
PO Box 883, Oxford, OX1 9PL, UK
PO Box 3985, New York, NY 10185-3985, USA
Email: info@ospreypublishing.com

Osprey Publishing is part of the Osprey Group.

© 2009 Osprey Publishing Ltd.

All rights reserved. Apart from any fair dealing for the purpose of private study, research,
criticism or review, as permitted under the Copyright, Designs and Patents Act, 1988,
no part of this publication may be reproduced, stored in a retrieval system, or transmitted
in any form or by any means, electronic, electrical, chemical, mechanical, optical,
photocopying, recording or otherwise, without the prior written permission of the
copyright owner. Enquiries should be addressed to the Publishers.

Transferred to digital print on demand 2014

First published 2009
1st impression 2009

Printed and bound in Great Britain.

A CIP catalogue record for this book is available from the British Library

ISBN: 978 1 84603 332 2

Page layout by Myriam Bell Design, France
Index by Alison Worthington
Originated by United Graphic Pte Ltd, Singapore
Typeset in Sabon and Myriad Pro

Author's acknowledgements
My grateful thanks to my wife Maggie, to Katherine Bracewell, and to
Caroline de Lambertye of the *Réunion des Musées Nationaux* for all their help.

The Woodland Trust
Osprey Publishing is supporting the Woodland Trust, the UK's leading woodland
conservation charity, by funding the dedication of trees.

www.ospreypublishing.com

CONTENTS

FRENCH *POILU* 1914–18

INTRODUCTION

When the French Army entered the war in 1914 it was just beginning to emerge from 20 years of disarray. A succession of political scandals – the Dreyfus affair (spying within the War Ministry), the *affaire des fiches* (the personal opinions and religious convictions of certain officers had been used to block their promotion), the disestablishment of the Catholic church (where the army had to intervene to keep the peace), and the use of the army in strikebreaking – combined with attempts to cut the two-year conscription period, or even to replace it with a Swiss-style militia, had all left the army in an uncertain state of morale and training. Why, the Kaiser enquired of Tsar Nicholas in 1913, did he wish to ally himself with France when 'the Frenchman is no longer capable of being a soldier'?

Ironically, it was Germany's attempt to intervene in Morocco in 1911 – the Agadir incident – that created a backlash of patriotism and anti-German feeling in France. Far from reducing the conscription period, the government increased it to three years in 1913. But the army that went to war in 1914 still had many weaknesses – it was poorly trained and poorly equipped, particularly in heavy artillery. This hardly mattered to the politicians, however, for they expected the war to last no longer than six months at most.

The 87e RI leaves its barracks in St Quentin on a route march. Following tradition, the regimental pioneers take the lead, followed by the drums and bugles. Since opportunities for training in the field were limited in peacetime France, such marches formed a significant part of a soldier's life. (Ian Sumner)

CHRONOLOGY

1914

August	Battle of the Frontiers
7–11 August	Battle of Alsace
20 August	Battle of Sarrebourg
20 August	Battle of Morhange
21–23 August	Battle of Charleroi
22–24 August	Battle of the Ardennes
24 Aug–6 Sept	First battle of Guise
24 Aug–16 Sept	Battles of the Haute–Meurthe and the Grand Couronné
25 Aug–11 Sept	Battle of the Mortagne
27–28 August	Battle of the Meuse
27 Aug–8 Sept	Battle and siege of Maubeuge
6–13 September	First battle of the Marne
15 September	First battle of the Aisne
15 Sept–19 Oct	Race to the Sea
21 Sept–13 Oct	Battle of Flirey
30 September	First battle of Picardie

Preceded by the regimental band, with flowers in their buttonholes and in the muzzles of their rifles, a regiment marches off to war from its garrison town in the Touraine. (Ian Sumner)

18 October	First battle of Flanders
22–30 October	Battle of the Yser
29 Oct–15 Nov	Battle of Ypres
17 Dec 1914–5 Jan	First battle of Artois
20 Dec 1914–16 Mar	First battle of Champagne

1915

5 Apr–5 May	First battle of Woëvre
9 May–18 June	Second battle of Artois
25 Sept–14 Oct	Third battle of Artois
25 Sept–16 Oct	Second battle of Champagne

1916

21 Feb–4 July	Defence of Verdun
1 July–26 Sept	Battle of the Somme
24 Oct–15 Dec	First Verdun offensive

1917

16 Apr–10 May	Second battle of the Aisne (Chemin des Dames)
17 April	Battle of Les Monts
31 July–10 Oct	Second battle of Flanders
20 Aug–8 Sept	Second Verdun offensive
23–27 Oct	Battle of Malmaison

The light infantry spirit is such that, although carrying a pack with blanket roll, tent section and tent pegs, this sergeant of the 3e *Bataillon de chasseurs à pied*, from St. Dié, still affects a dashing air. (Ian Sumner)

1918

21–31 March	Second battle of Picardie
4–16 May	Third battle of Flanders
27 May–1 June	Third battle of the Aisne
9–11 June	Battle of Matz
15 July	Fourth battle of Champagne
18–29 July	Battles of Soissonais–Ourcq
18 July–6 Aug	Second battle of the Marne
29 July–8 Aug	Battle of Tardenois
8–17 August	Battle of Montdidier
8–29 August	Third battle of Picardie
17–29 August	Second battle of Noyon
29 Aug–20 Sept	Advance to the Hindenburg Line
26 Sept–15 Oct	Battle of Champagne–Argonne

Two Algerian *tirailleurs* at the wartime depot of Aix-en-Provence. The regiments of the North African garrison sent individual battalions to France, where they were formed into provisional *régiments de marche*. One of the men shown here was in the 3rd Battalion, 6e *Tirailleurs*, later part of the 7e *Régiment de marche*, along with battalions from five other regiments. (Ian Sumner)

A trainload of foreign volunteers (note the Swiss flag on the left) leave a major city, perhaps Paris, for their depot. (Ian Sumner)

JOINING UP

The French Army was manned by conscription, and every 20-year-old male was liable for three years' service with the colours. Until 1905, not every man of the qualifying age was called up: selection was by ballot of those eligible to serve, and there were many exemptions. After that date, nearly all the exemptions were abolished, and service was virtually obligatory.

Every January, a list of men eligible for service by age was posted in each commune. Those listed had to appear before a board consisting of a general officer, the departmental prefect and other representatives of local government. Every man was measured and weighed by a medical officer: some had their call-up immediately postponed because of lack of stature, and more were then excluded on grounds of congenital infirmity. Others were rejected on more arbitrary grounds – a tattooed face could be sufficient. In January 1915, one board was considering a man who was covered in tattoos from head to foot. Rejecting him, the medical officer remarked jokingly that 'there's no more room'; the man, who had already seen service with the brutal *Bataillon d'Infanterie Légère d'Afrique* (BILA), replied, 'There's room for a bullet', and he was passed fit for service. He was soon proved right about the bullet, too; he was wounded at Carency just four months later. Convicted felons were called up along with the rest. Those who found themselves in prison when their call-up was due were allowed to serve out their sentence and were then sent to the BILA.

In a tradition which dated almost from the beginning of conscription at the end of the 18th century, those selected by ballot for service each year were given a big send-off by their home town or village, dressed in distinctive costumes with ribbons and flowers, and given a special flag to carry. Although this custom did not die out completely in the era of universal liability, it did become rather more muted. Yet it never disappeared entirely, even during wartime. Captain J. C. Dunn, in his book *The War the Infantry Knew*, notes in March 1918, 'Going on leave, I saw in Steenwerck the latest class of French conscripts leaving home for their depots. Dressed in their Sunday best, beflowered, beribboned, beflagged, befuddled, they were calling at every friend's house and being given liquor. Poor boys.'

Most men went into the infantry. Restrictions in size and weight limited those who could serve in the cavalry, whilst service in the artillery and engineers was normally reserved for those who had worked on the railways or in public works, shipyards and telecommunications. The infantry was, therefore, composed primarily of men from an agricultural background, although 20 per cent were shop assistants, small craftsmen and factory workers, and a further 5 per cent clerks or teachers. After their service with the 'active' army, conscripts passed into the Reserve for a period of 11 years. On mobilization, each infantry regiment and each light infantry (*chasseur à pied*) battalion raised a Reserve unit, which was intended to take the field

A colour party of the 57e RI, which recruited in Libourne and Rochefort. All the escort have been decorated with the Croix de Guerre. Eventually, the regiment would receive the same honour, with a green and red lanyard decorating the colours, and worn by the men on their left shoulders. (Ian Sumner)

but only to man garrisons and lines of communication. In the event, these Reserve divisions had to take their place in the line alongside those made up of serving soldiers. As Joffre said in 1915, 'There is no such thing as Reserves.'

On completing his service in the Reserves, each man passed into the Territorials for a further seven years, and then into the Territorial Reserves for a final seven years, making 28 years' service in total. The Territorials were intended purely as local defence units and were only recalled to the colours in times of war. In an emergency, as during the Race to the Sea in September 1914, some Territorial regiments saw action as well, but for most of the war, those not guarding lines of communication were used as works battalions – making and maintaining trench systems, roads and railway lines.

Regiments were created on a local basis. Every regiment drew its recruits from a specific number of local government areas (*arrondissements*), while divisions and army corps were formed from regiments from the same Military Region. Like the British Pals battalions, this provided a source both of strength and of weakness. Soldiers were able to serve with men from their own immediate locality, an advantage at a time when country accents could be difficult for any outsider to understand. However, heavy casualties would have a disproportionate effect on a relatively small area, and there were other disadvantages to this system. In 1907, the 17e *Régiment d'Infanterie* (RI), whose depot was in Béziers, was ordered to quell unrest amongst the local wine growers. Faced with men who undoubtedly included friends and relatives, the regiment mutinied, and over 500 soldiers were sent to Tunisia as punishment.

Peacetime training was conducted almost entirely within the regiment. A shortage of large training grounds, and a shortage of money, meant that field exercises were few. Larger formations conducted manoeuvres on a four-yearly cycle. In the first two years exercises were conducted at brigade level; in the third year at army corps level; and in the fourth year at army level. The result was that no conscript would ever serve through the whole of the training cycle. The training provided for reservists was even more limited. They were recalled for only 40 days each year, in two periods; the first of 23 days, the second of 17, and a shortage of suitable exercise grounds meant that much of this time was spent in barracks, rather than in the field. The Territorials had one nine-day training period a year; the Territorial Reserves one day only.

Mobilization was ordered on 1 August 1914. The classes of 1896

Map showing the boundaries of the army corps regions. The 19th Corps was based in North Africa. The Paris Military Region contributed divisions to the 3rd, 4th and 5th Corps.

to 1910 (men between 24 and 38 years of age) were called up immediately, and some 4,300 trains transported them to their depots and war stations. The classes of 1892 to 1895 followed in December 1914, those of 1889 to 1891 in March–April 1915, and those of 1886 to 1888 in the following year. Calling up the older classes, destined for service in the rear areas, was designed to allow fit young men to be sent to the front. Yet that alone would not be enough. The class of 1914 was called up early, in August of that year, and the class of 1915 followed in December 1914. The class of 1916 was called up in April 1915, that of 1917 in January 1916, that of 1918 in April–May 1917, and finally that of 1919 in April 1918.

In addition to the metropolitan army, which served almost wholly on French soil (conscripts were prevented by law from serving abroad in peacetime), a number of regiments which garrisoned French possessions abroad, particularly in Africa and Indochina, could also be called upon to serve in France. Most importantly, these regiments were unique in having combat experience, albeit only of colonial warfare, and had thus attracted officers and volunteers who were unwilling to serve in a dusty mainland garrison town and had instead sought out active service.

Some of these regiments were raised for service in North Africa – in the infantry, the *zouaves*, *tirailleurs* and Foreign Legion. The *tirailleurs* were raised from the indigenous peoples of Algeria and Tunisia, the *zouaves* from Frenchmen. Only the *zouaves* were raised from conscripts; the other regiments were all made up of volunteers. During the war, these regiments had to maintain a garrison in Algeria, Tunisia and Morocco, and consequently sent to France only individual battalions, grouped together as provisional *régiments de marche*. The North African regiments also included a small number of cavalry units – *chasseurs d'Afrique* and *spahis*.

The other, larger, group was that formed by the Colonial regiments. Raised from French citizens and, in contrast to the metropolitan army, all made up of volunteers, these regiments served as the garrisons of French colonies, largely in western and central Africa and in Indochina. They were originally part of the navy, only transferring to army control in 1900, and retained a separate administrative structure throughout the war (indeed, until 1958). Their main depots were in the principal French naval ports –

Every cavalry division included a battalion of *chasseur* cyclists. When in action, the bicycle was folded in two and carried on the rider's back. (Ian Sumner)

Some senior officers, notably General Mangin, enthusiastically supported the extensive use of black African soldiers on the Western Front. However, they were not suited to the conditions, especially in winter, and had to be supported by white battalions. Some battalions had to be retained in west Africa (here, Fort Bonnier in Timbuctoo), serving in German West Africa and against the Senussi Revolt. (Ian Sumner)

Cherbourg, Brest, Toulon, Rochefort – and so they were on hand to take the field in 1914. Battalions of indigenous African and Indochinese troops also formed part of the Colonial organization. These units were not present during the opening campaigns in France, but as casualties mounted it became impossible to ignore them; indeed, the manpower crisis that occurred in the later stages of the war forced the introduction of conscription in West Africa.

All armies and corps contained a significant cavalry component whose intended role was quickly rendered insignificant by trench warfare. Over the winter of 1914–15 most cavalry regiments had created a squadron for service on foot. But by 1916 the infantry needed more men to replace casualties, and the artillery needed horses, so six *cuirassier* regiments, with drafts from other mounted troops, were converted to infantry, forming two divisions of *cuirassiers à pied*.

The peacetime army had a strength of 817,000 men, augmented on mobilization to 2,944,000. In all, some 7,800,000 served with the colours during the war, around 80 per cent of a total population of 9,697,000 men of eligible age. To these can be added 229,000 volunteers and 608,000 Colonial troops.

In addition to these fighting troops, workers were brought in from abroad to act as replacements in industry or to serve in works battalions in the rear areas; around 200,000 men from the colonies (including 50,000 Indochinese) as well as 100,000 foreigners (including 13,000 Chinese) and some 82,000 prisoners of war were employed in one way or another.

Joining the Regiment

Every infantry regiment comprised three peacetime battalions of four companies each, numbered 1 to 12. At mobilization, calling up the reserves enabled the formation of a Reserve regiment of two battalions, which took the number of the parent regiment plus 200 (thus the 1er RI formed the 201e). Its battalions were numbered 5 and 6, and its companies numbered from 17 to 24. A peacetime recruit, joining his regiment in October, would spend around two months learning the basics of military life. Training at squad level began around the middle of December of each year. Exercises in company strength followed in mid-March, and continued until the summer and the manoeuvres season.

All the men of the five field armies had been assembled by 10 August, the Reserve divisions by the 13th, and the units charged with defending Paris by the 15th. Recalled reservists were processed in the shortest time: Abel Castel, for example, reporting at the depot of the 35e RI at Belfort on the morning of 1 August, was on his way to join his regiment that same afternoon. The 275e RI at Romans was assembled in two days, issued with its food and ammunition the next day, and on its way to the front within the week. But these were men who had completed their service only recently and were expected to have retained at least some of their training.

The class of 1914 was thrown into the field quickly, probably too quickly, in order to replace casualties. In the 74e RI, a report of late 1914 noted, 'Instruction in combat is very rudimentary. Information on the present conflict appears to be totally unknown at the depot. The men claim that they only fired their rifles once a week. The volunteers from Alsace do not know how to shoot.' Roland Dorgelès managed to join the 39e RI without any training at all, simply by insisting that he be sent directly to the front.

For new recruits in subsequent classes, the process was slower. The 'missing' companies of each regiment (13 to 16) became the regimental depot, and were used for the basic training of recruits. Further companies, numbered from 25 to 28, formed a 7th Battalion, which occupied camps situated in the countryside around the depot towns, and conducted field exercises. With this part of his training complete, the recruit then transferred to the 9th Battalion (there was no 8th Battalion) of a regiment from the same Military Region, formed by combining drafts from the local regiments; until 1916 these were also known as Divisional Depots, and then Divisional Instruction Centres. These 9th battalions were stationed in the rear areas. They helped acclimatize new troops to service at the front (usually through providing working parties), and also provided specialist training, for example as signallers,

A group from the 89e *Régiment d'Infanterie Territoriale*, of Quincampoix, Brittany, in 1915. They are wearing a typical mixture of pre-war and wartime clothing, including tunics and trousers in corduroy, and two different types of horizon blue greatcoat. This unit saw action during the Race for the Sea, but these men are guarding lines of communication; other regiments were employed on trench digging or road maintenance. (Ian Sumner)

pioneers or machine gunners. From here, the trained soldier would be sent to the front as part of a draft of reinforcements.

The experience of Henri Latécoère is typical. After reporting to his depot (that of the 107e RI in Angoulême) when the class of 1917 was called up in January 1916, he spent five months in barracks and two months in a camp completing his basic training, before forming part of a draft for the front in August 1916. His first posting was not to a combat regiment, but to a training unit, the 9th Battalion of the 138e RI, another infantry regiment in his division. Here, he underwent his advanced training, to make him ready for the front. In November 1916, he was posted as a replacement to a Divisional Depot of the 3e DI, a completely different division. In Latécoère's case, he then had to wait a further four months until the class of 1917 was considered old enough to serve at the front.

As Latécoère's story shows, a recruit was not necessarily posted to his local regiment, but was sent where the need was greatest. While many regiments managed to maintain at least a regional, if not a purely local, character throughout the course of the war, this was impossible for those with depots situated in the towns and cities of the north and east, by then under German occupation. By 1917, for example, a typical squad in a nominally Picard regiment, the 128e RI, was led by a corporal from just outside Paris, who commanded two Charentais, from western France, a Picard, a Norman, a Breton, and one man from the Ardennes.

Serving soldiers, reservists or conscripts all received a big send-off when their regiment or draft left the barracks, usually for the local railway station. With the bands playing famous old tunes like 'Sambre et Meuse' or 'Chant du Départ', cheering crowds gathered, offering the soldiers flowers or even kisses, sometimes singing the 'Marseillaise' or the popular song 'Quand Madelon'. The soldiers responded in kind, or, in the case of the chasseurs, with their own song, 'Sidi Brahim'. This remained common practice, even in 1916. 'A moving moment,' recalled Latécoère. 'We are greeted with cheers by bystanders. The bugles at the head of the column sound the march.'

OPPOSITE
There may be duckboards at the bottom of this trench, but there is no revetting on the sides. British troops who took over French sections of the line were sometimes appalled by the 'relaxed' attitude to trench construction shown by their allies. The officer on the left is from the *chasseurs à pied*, as revealed by the hunting horn badge on his helmet, and the dark blue trousers. His *vareuse* has an integral belt.
(Ian Sumner)

As in Britain, the number of men under arms allowed women to take jobs previously done by men. Here the craftsmen and women of the depot of the 26e RA, at Le Mans, pose for a photo.
(Ian Sumner)

Uniform

In the late 19th and early 20th centuries, the army, as an institution, had come under attack from both Left and Right. In consequence, much-needed reforms had often been sacrificed on the altar of political expediency. Several attempts to design a camouflage uniform for the army had all failed. The first of these, the bluish-grey *tenue Boër* of 1902–03, complete with slouch hat, was rejected on the grounds that its colour was too close to that worn by the Italian Army; the second, the beige-blue uniform of 1903–06, and the third, the grey-green *tenue réséda* of 1911, were turned down because they were too like German uniforms. To complicate matters further, any proposal to abolish the red trousers of the infantry, and replace them with something more suited to modern warfare, was condemned as somehow un-French. A project that included a blue-grey uniform, promoted by the military artists Edouard Détaille and Georges Scott, got no further than the artist's drawings.

Evidence from the Balkan Wars, however, showed just how vital a camouflage uniform had become, and a fourth trial was undertaken in 1912. On this occasion, the cloth involved was *drap tricolore*, a fabric composed of alternate blue, white and red threads, and it was judged successful until it was noticed that the manufacturers of the red dye used in the material were all German. Nevertheless, the project went ahead – without the red threads – and, in the summer of 1914, the famous horizon blue (a mixture of 35 per cent white thread, 15 per cent dark blue and 50 per cent light blue) was born.

Deliveries had not yet begun by the outbreak of war, and the French Army entered the conflict wearing a uniform little different from that of 1870. This was the uniform that became the scapegoat for French defeats – the red trousers were too visible on the battlefield, it was claimed, making the soldiers

SOLDAT, 15E *RÉGIMENT D'INFANTERIE*, SEPTEMBER 1914

At first glance there is little to distinguish this soldier of 1914 (**1**) from his counterpart of 1870. Attempts to replace the red and blue uniform with more modern patterns, or to provide lighter equipment, failed before the conservatism of politicians and high command alike. Rising international tension from 1911 onwards initially provided an ideal excuse to postpone trials of new matériel, but eventually the approaching war gave the army the impetus it needed to introduce a new uniform, and manufacture of greatcoats in the new horizon blue began in the summer of 1914. Other short-term measures were also taken: officers' rank badges, worn on the sleeve, were abandoned in September 1914, and it became compulsory to wear the blue cap cover that October. By the end of the month, patterns in blue or brown cloth or corduroy were temporarily replacing the red trousers.

The greatcoat, originally introduced in 1877, had always been unsatisfactory, for the low collar gave no protection against the cold, and wearing the equipment hampered access to the pockets. Nevertheless, this was the first item to be made in the new colour. The peacetime version was officially abandoned in December 1914.

The pack (**2**) was introduced in 1893, and was made of leather over a wooden frame. Each of the three front cartridge pouches held four packets, each packet holding eight rounds, with a further three packets in the rear pouch. Each man also carried four more packets, either in his pack or in the pockets of his greatcoat, giving a total of 120 rounds. A full pack weighed 7.8kg, and the rifle, ammunition and remaining personal equipment increased his load to 24.76kg. Tools and mess tins might add between another 0.5kg and 1.22kg, and if the man carried a tent section as well, then his total *barda* (an Arab word from France's campaigns in Africa, meaning 'equipment', but with overtones of 'burden') could be as much as 28.42kg.

Our soldier's underwear consisted of a shirt (which could double as a nightshirt) (**3**) and drawers (**4**) in cotton ticking, and, introduced only in 1909, a pair of white woollen socks (**5**).

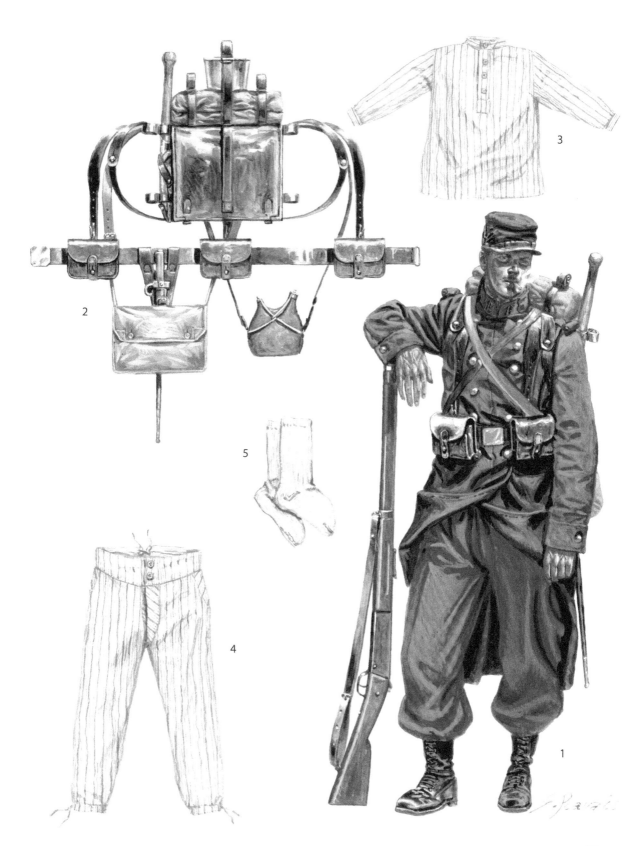

2

3

5

4

1

'*Les poilus de la 51e*': the photo is dated 1916, but none of these men have been issued with the full horizon blue uniform. The two men in the light-coloured uniform in the back row are wearing the canvas jacket and trousers adopted as a fatigue uniform. Regimental bandsmen served as stretcher-bearers, but buglers remained with their companies. (Ian Sumner)

easy targets. The autumn and winter of 1914 saw a number of measures rushed into service, replacing the red trousers with patterns in blue or dark brown. However, the more likely explanation for French losses lay in the tactics employed and in structural weaknesses in the army as a whole – lack of reconnaissance, too few officers and NCOs, insufficient artillery support – rather than simply in the clothing worn by the soldiers.

With preference allotted to front line units, horizon blue made its debut in the early spring of 1915. The first items to be made in the new fabric were greatcoats, followed by trousers and then the tunic. The new uniform was similar in appearance for all arms of service, the only difference lying in the collar patches of both tunic and greatcoat, and in the piping down the outside of the trouser leg. Rank was displayed in short coloured strips on the cuffs. The trousers were tucked into puttees.

Headgear consisted of a képi. The original pattern of 1914 was worn under a cover of blue cotton to reduce its visibility, but this too was replaced by a version in horizon blue. The steel Adrian helmet made its first appearance towards the end of the same year, replacing a steel skull cap worn under the képi, but it was not widely used until 1916. In reply to an officer who had proposed that a helmet be introduced, Joffre wrote optimistically, 'We will not have the time to make them, I will break the Boche within two months', but his prediction proved sadly wide of the mark. The first examples of the helmet were painted with a gloss finish, but a matt version was introduced in late 1916. For off-duty wear, the helmet was replaced by a horizon blue *bonnet de police*.

Colonial and African units, however, wore a khaki uniform. The ready availability of khaki cloth from the UK may have played a part in this decision, but as the war progressed, French- and American-made items were also introduced, with the result that three slightly different shades of khaki were all eventually in use.

'Everything made for the soldier,' grumbled Henri Barbusse, famous for his novel *Le Feu*, and a member of the 231e RI, 'is ordinary, ugly and of poor quality.' So it is hardly surprising that the soldier supplemented his regulation uniform with all manner of items, dispatched by loved ones or obtained by the man himself by fair means or foul. Sheep and goat skins, even rabbit or hare, woollen scarves, balaclavas and pullovers in different colours, waterproofs, rags wound around the boots for warmth – all were adopted with enthusiasm. 'Yesterday's man about town is no longer recognizable in this hairy, bearded combatant, plastered in mud and filth, infested with fleas, covered by sheepskins, and wearing deep trench boots,' as one army doctor observed.

Cold and rain always posed problems. In the hills of the Vosges, winter temperatures could fall so low that even the wine and bread froze. The winter of 1914–15 was particularly hard, since a trench system, with its sheltering dug-outs, had not yet been fully constructed. However, later winters were little better. 'We struggled against the cold the best we could,' recalled one soldier. 'Our cap protected our ears and forehead; a scarf was wound around the lower part of our faces; only our eyes were visible. On top of this heap of cloth was perched our helmet, a shaky tin roof, and over that, where possible, a blanket, which fell across our shoulders, making us look like a sentry box.'

Rain meant mud: *boue, mélasse, gadoue, gadouille, mouise, mouscaille* – there were so many names for the substance that was central to the life of every front line soldier. 'Communications trenches are little more than sewers of mixed water and urine. The trench little more than a sheet of water. Its sides collapse with a wet, sliding noise as you pass. And we are all transformed into clay statues, with mud up to our mouths.' Mud got everywhere, but it was particularly dangerous when it penetrated the breeches

The men of the *chasseurs alpins*, the specialist mountain troops, carried the same pack as other infantry, but also the extra burden of snowshoes and an alpenstock. These battalions spent most of the war on the Vosges Front. (Ian Sumner)

A group of the 55e RI pose with their Chauchat. Some men wear a horizon blue 'alpine' beret that was briefly issued in 1916. It was unpopular with the Alpine troops, who did not like to see their distinctive headgear worn by the whole army, and it was unpopular with everyone else because it was so big, and so difficult to stow away. It was replaced by the fore-and-aft *bonnet de police*, which several other men are seen wearing here. (Ian Sumner)

of the infantry's firearms. In the wet spring of 1915, Maurice Genevoix recorded that two trenches were lost to the enemy because the mud had put so many rifles out of action.

Water was scarce in the front line, and water for shaving scarcer still. The alleged hairiness of the soldiers gave rise to their most enduring nickname, '*poilu*' ('hairy one'), but in the front line, this was regarded as yet more journalistic nonsense in a war that had already seen too much. The traditional nickname of the infantry was '*les biffins*' – 'rag-and-bone men'. To each other, they were '*les bonhommes*' – 'the lads', or, as war weariness overtook them, '*les pauvres cons du front*' or 'PCDF' – 'the poor bastards at the front'.

The Croix de Guerre was introduced on 8 April 1915, as a distinction for all men Mentioned in Orders. The ribbon bore a bronze star for a mention in regimental or brigade orders, a silver star for divisional orders, a gilt star for

Marshal Foch decorates an Algerian *tirailleur* at the victory celebrations of 1919. Note the crescent on the finial of the *fanion*, and the Hand of Fatima device on the flag itself; both were distinctive symbols of Algerian regiments. (Ian Sumner)

corps orders, or a bronze palm leaf for army orders. Five bronze stars were exchanged for a silver palm leaf. Awards could also be given to any regiment which had received sufficient citations, in the form of a lanyard in the colours of the ribbon of the Croix de Guerre, Médaille Militaire or even the Légion d'Honneur. The rationale behind these distinctions was to provide a tangible reward for men who had distinguished themselves on active service. But, some wondered, where lay the value of a reward that could just as well be given to a soldier for a bold feat of arms under fire, as to the man who simply set up the army's Camouflage Service and never got near the front line?

A column of infantry, encumbered by their packs, march through a town early in the war. (Ian Sumner)

EQUIPMENT AND WEAPONS

In the army of 1914, experience of campaigning in Africa and elsewhere in the colonies had created the tradition that a soldier carried as much as possible on his person. The leather straps of his personal equipment supported three leather cartridge pouches (one either side of the belt buckle, and a third in the small of the wearer's back), a leather pack and a bayonet frog; across his shoulders was a canvas haversack and a 1-litre water bottle (later replaced by a 2-litre version). In addition to his own equipment, each man carried one of the squad's six cooking pots, or one of the company's tools (pickaxe, spade, shears or axe). Depending therefore on what he was carrying, and whether or not he was carrying a tent section, the total weight lay between 25kg (55lb) and 28kg (62lb).

It was units of the Tenth Army in the Ypres sector that, in April 1915, suffered the unfortunate distinction of being the first to experience a gas attack. At that time there was no defence against its effects, and an enemy breakthrough was halted only at great cost. By August, however, a mask was being distributed to front line troops. The mask itself, the P or P2, was rudimentary, consisting of nothing more than a treated cloth pad worn over the nose and mouth and secured to the head by cotton tape. This was

sufficient for up to 2 hours' protection. A separate pair of goggles was also issued. Both mask and goggles were kept in a small waterproof package which could be attached to the wearer's personal equipment (also useful for storing tobacco!). They were supplemented in some units by hoods of treated fabric, but technical and manufacturing problems meant that these were not universally adopted.

Soldiers found the P2 difficult to put on quickly and hard to adapt to the contours of the face – factors held to account for the near success of a German attack south-east of Rheims in October 1915. Nor was it of any value against phosgene, first used on 26 November 1915, near Verdun, and from January 1916, a new mask, the TN, was introduced. The TN consisted of a conical mask with elasticated straps and a separate pair of goggles. They were carried in a small oval tin, suspended from the waistbelt, and provided protection for up to 4 hours against chlorine gas, and up to 5 hours against phosgene. A further modification, making the goggles part of the mask, was then introduced in the autumn of 1916, and this new version, the M2, remained the standard pattern until 1918. The performance of the M2 improved on that of the TN, making it possible to survive for more than 4 hours against chlorine,

and also making it better than contemporary German masks. From February 1918, the M2 was replaced by the ARS 1917, which was closer in appearance to German patterns, but included improved filtering.

Personal Weapons

The basic infantry weapon was the 8mm Lebel rifle, originally designed in 1886, and modified in 1896. Although generally a robust and accurate weapon, the Lebel suffered from one major defect – the design of the magazine. This was filled by pushing a maximum of eight single rounds down a tube bored in the fore-end. As each bullet was consumed, the Lebel's centre of gravity changed, requiring every shot to be carefully aimed. Reloading was necessarily slow, and the gun was over-long. The Lebel was an obsolescent weapon, much inferior to the Mausers and Mannlichers carried by the enemy.

From 1915, it was replaced by the 1907 Berthier. This was a lengthened version of the standard cavalry carbine, originally intended for Colonial troops. The particular advantage of the Berthier was that its ammunition was loaded in three-round clips, and a change to five-round clips in 1916 brought further improvement. It took some time to introduce the Berthier because so many Lebels were already in stock, but the class of 1917 was armed with the new weapon from the beginning. Lebels, rather more robust than the newer Berthiers, continued in use with rifle grenades (see below); others, with a telescopic sight attached, were used by snipers. A small number of fully automatic FA17 rifles were also issued in 1917–18, but they suffered from a number of defects that severely restricted their actual use.

In 1914, each man carried 88 rounds on his person: 32 in each front pouch, contained in four paper packets, and 24 in the rear pouch. However, the regiments belonging to the 6e, 7e and 20e Corps, stationed near the eastern frontier with Germany, were issued with 120 rounds per man. In wartime conditions, this tended to be the general level of issue, although the

OPPOSITE ABOVE

A squad of *zouaves* on patrol. All are carrying their full pack, including cooking vessels – a practice which started on campaign in North Africa. The sergeant on the right wears a marksmanship badge on his sleeve. (Ian Sumner)

OPPOSITE BELOW

A photo reportedly depicting French troops in action, but probably taken on peacetime manoeuvres. The firing line has been formed, with the men in pairs, lying in scrapes behind the excavated earth, which has been reinforced by their packs. In the background, a platoon waits its turn to be fed into the firing line. (Ian Sumner)

BELOW

A squad of the 29e *Régiment d'Infanterie* (RI), whose depot was at Autun in Burgundy. The length of the rifle with its bayonet fixed is quite apparent. Note the roll on the greatcoat shoulder, to support the straps of the pack. (Ian Sumner)

23

Bombers, armed with Foug grenades, in the trenches in the Woëvre. (Photo RMN Anon).

regulations for the Berthier specified only 84 (i.e. 28 three-round clips). The company baggage held a reserve of a further 112 rounds per man.

Accompanying the rifle was an 1886 pattern bayonet. This weapon was long (45cm/18in), of cruciform cross-section, and very slender, which meant it had a tendency to snap. The bayonet was the object of much mythologizing, and even acquired a nickname, 'Rosalie', from a popular song of the first August of the war. The bayonet charge, with colours flying and bugles sounding, remained a gleam in the eyes of those, journalists and others, who never saw the front. Jean-Norton Cru, who served with the 250e RI, and later made an extensive study of wartime memoirs, was dismissive of the notion. In a typically grumpy aside, he noted that, since bayonets were routinely fixed prior to combat, there was no more reason to call an attack a bayonet charge than a puttee attack. There was little hand-to-hand fighting during the course of the war; the bayonet was more useful for opening tins, or as a hook from which to hang equipment.

B WEAPONS

The Lebel rifle that accompanied the Army to war proved unsatisfactory, and from 1915 was replaced by the Berthier. The Berthier's principal advantage was that it was designed to fire clips of ammunition, rather than single shots – but the clips only contained three rounds each. The version shown here (**1**), with a five-round capacity (**2**), was introduced in 1916. The bayonet (**3**) also underwent slight modification, reducing the size of the quillons, to prevent it tangling with barbed wire.

Research into automatic rifles had begun as early as the 1890s, and a design was also produced by the team behind the Chauchat machine gun. Their FA17 (also known as the RSC) automatic rifle (**4**) was first introduced onto the Western Front in 1917, at the rate of eleven per company, with preference given to the best shots. But the weapon was over-long, over-heavy, and like the Chauchat, prone to mechanical failures. After the war, development of such weapons was abandoned.

Machine gunners were armed with a 7.65mm Ruby automatic pistol (**5**) for their own defence. It was widely used, but lacked stopping power. From 1917, the Star pistol began to replace it, but the Ruby never went completely out of use.

Hand grenades, once the specialist weapon of engineers, soon became an important item in the infantry's armoury, progressing from the crude F2 hand grenade (**6**), through the P4 (**7**) to the OF (**8**) and the OP1 (**9**).

The first gas masks (**10**), introduced in 1915, consisted simply of a cloth pad impregnated with chemicals, carried in an oilcloth pouch.

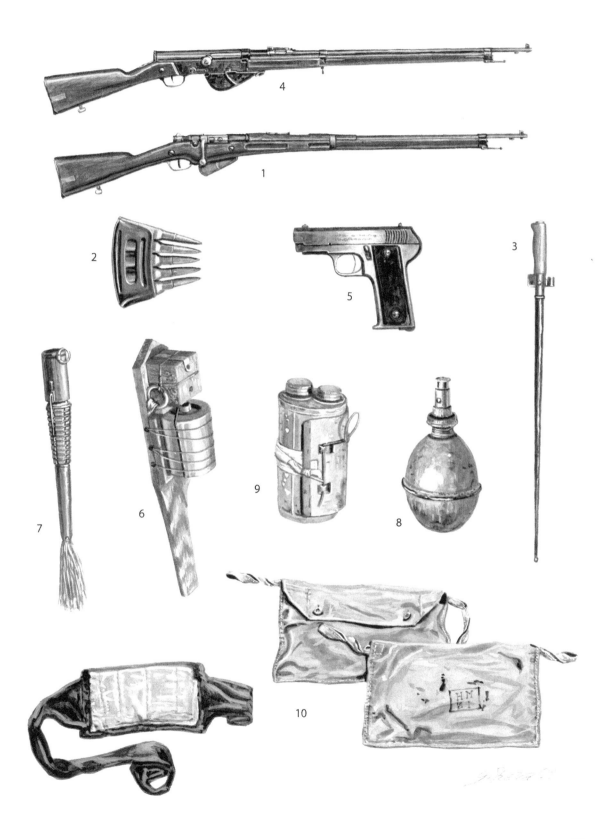

Officers (as well as cadets and *adjudants*) carried a pistol, either the regulation 1892 revolver, or one of any number of makes such as Colt, privately purchased. Swords were normally left with the company baggage, particularly after the first few months of the war, although an account of the 221e RI at Verdun in July 1916 describes a captain trying to launch a counter-attack, sabre in hand. Many officers replaced their sword with a walking stick, British-style, but since this still rather obviously identified their status, they continued to suffer heavy casualties. Some junior officers carried the same rifles as their men, but that was a personal decision.

Hand Grenades

The nature of combat at the front saw the hand grenade come into its own. At the outbreak of war, the regulations governing the use of hand grenades dated from 1847, while the grenade itself still came with an exterior fuse. The first attempts at replacements consisted of nothing more than small explosive charges attached to pieces of wood. A more modern-looking weapon was the Besozzi grenade, approximately the size and shape of a lemon, introduced in early 1915. But the Besozzi still used an exterior fuse, which had to be lit with a slow match (or, more often, the bomber's pipe!) – a task requiring some concentration in the middle of No Man's Land. The Besozzi was replaced by the F1, lit instead by striking the exterior fuse. However, the cardboard tube that contained the fuse provided little protection from the damp of the trenches, and the grenade all too often failed to explode. The F1 was quickly followed by the pear-shaped P1, whose explosive content was too weak to shatter the shell effectively. Three

A group of graduates of the Machine Gun School at Le Ruchard; all are northerners, from the 85e (whose pre-war garrison was Cosne-sur-Loire), 87e (St Quentin), 89e (Sens), 91e (Mézieres) and 95e (Bourges) RIs. The courses run by the school were intended for officers and NCOs who would command machine gun detachments; the training of machine gun crews took place within the regiment. (Ian Sumner)

more P-series grenades, numbered 2 to 4, were then produced. They were closer in design to German stick grenades, with long handles and ribbons to help stabilize them in flight.

It was not until 1916 that an efficient grenade, the Billant (a modified version of the F1), was finally produced. This retained the lemon shape of the Besozzi, but was fired, like the British Mills bomb, by pulling a wire pin and allowing a lever to rise and thus ignite the fuse. However, the French habit of carrying these grenades loose in a haversack, allied to poor-quality workmanship, meant that the levers and pins easily became entangled and premature explosions were common.

A small number of special grenades were introduced in 1916 for clearing trenches and dug-outs. These contained either tear-gas, phosphorous or 'calorite', a compound that burned at nearly 3,000°C, and was used to destroy anything metallic. None of these special grenades, however, was produced in any quantity.

More significant was the introduction of the Vivien-Bessières (VB) rifle grenade. A number of earlier 'home-made' attempts, involving catapults, had been made to find a method of projecting grenades into enemy trenches – none of them truly successful. The VB was a 'bullet through' weapon. Once a grenade had been placed in the special muzzle cup, and the rifle placed with its butt on the ground, a fired bullet struck the grenade and ignited the 8-second fuse. The maximum range of the VB was 170 metres (186 yards), much further than a man could throw, and it became a centrepiece of the new platoon tactics of 1916.

Machine Guns

The first machine gun introduced into the French Army was the 1897 Hotchkiss. Problems with overheating led to the development of a number of competitors, but none could match the Hotchkiss, and one, the 1905 Puteaux, was markedly less effective. Attempts by the Government Arsenal at St Etienne to improve the Puteaux succeeded only in over-complicating it, making a poor design worse still. Nevertheless, it was introduced into the

The accurate and powerful 37mm infantry gun, here shown in a post-war photograph. Wheels could be attached for moving over rough round, and there was also a gun shield, but the weapon was heavy enough without the extras.
(Ian Sumner)

'Troops,' commented a French training manual, 'can only be trusted for an assault when their hearts and legs have been trained for it.' Training focused on the assault, and its main aim was to develop qualities of agility, aggressive spirit, boldness and cohesion. The bayonet fencing exercise shown here remained part of the training curriculum throughout the war, although relatively few men were actually wounded by an enemy bayonet. Recruits went on from this exercise to an obstacle course, 100 to 200 metres in length, where dummies were hung, either concealed or in the open. But there was much more to hand-to-hand combat training than merely learning to stab an opponent. 'It is a mistake,' continued the manual, 'to think that … it is sufficient to rush head down and bayonet fixed … In fact, the close proximity of man to man, the unforeseen appearance of one or two enemies, or the least surprise, disconcerts the soldiers unless they have been accustomed to be astonished at nothing, to keep cool and determined and to face every unforeseen circumstance.'

army as a replacement for the Hotchkiss. Exposed to the conditions of the Western Front, the weapon quickly revealed its shortcomings, and it was banished to the colonies, to be replaced by the faithful Hotchkiss.

The Hotchkiss was not fed by rounds held in fabric belts, but instead employed short aluminium trays containing 24 rounds each. On grounds of economy, it used the same 8mm rounds as the Lebel rifle. Its rate of fire was between 400 and 600 rounds per minute, with a range of 1,800m (1.2 miles) direct and 4,000m (2.5 miles) indirect. Even though it was air-cooled, and did not therefore include a water jacket, the Hotchkiss was not a light weapon – the gun itself weighed 24kg (53lb), and its tripod base about the same. The ammunition was carried in wooden boxes, each containing 12 strips (i.e. 288 rounds), weighing 12kg (26lb) each.

The result, although weighty and cumbersome, was an excellent weapon. At Verdun, one section of two guns was isolated by the German advance and held off the enemy for ten days and nights, during which the two guns are supposed to have fired in excess of 75,000 rounds. Both were in excellent order when relief finally arrived, and, almost as importantly for their crews, had not used any of their precious water.

The Hotchkiss and St Etienne were too heavy to carry into the assault, so the French had also looked to develop a weapon that would incorporate the machine gun's volume of fire into the attack in a more easily portable form. The result was the Chauchat.

The Chauchat (more properly the Chauchat-Sutter-Ribeyrolles-Gladiator, after its inventors and manufacturers) was developed as part of a pre-war programme to produce an automatic rifle rather than a machine gun. Chauchat conceived his new weapon as something analogous to an artillery piece, able to lay down a barrage of fire at enemy targets. Indeed this volume of fire was considered almost more important than the shot-by-shot accuracy of the weapon.

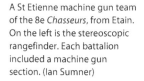

A St Etienne machine gun team of the 8e *Chasseurs*, from Etain. On the left is the stereoscopic rangefinder. Each battalion included a machine gun section. (Ian Sumner)

The colours and *fanions* of the Moroccan Division – the RMLE, the 4e and 7e *Régiments de Tirailleurs Indigènes* and the 8e *Régiment de marche de Zouaves*. On the right is the *fanion* of the 7e, with its powerful motto, 'Fearless, Pitiless'. (Ian Sumner)

To produce the barrage required, the weapon was designed to be fired at the walk, with the firer and his number two side by side. To keep up the volume of fire, the number two had to know when to change magazines with the minimum of delay, so the magazine was made with openings on the side, allowing him to keep an eye on the ammunition consumption. This may have worked well on a test range, but in the field it was disastrous. The difficulties of maintaining accurate fire while walking under fire over broken ground are obvious. Mud and dust entered the gun's firing mechanism; the magazines were too easy to damage when carried in their pouches; the spring was too weak. Moreover, the bipod was flimsy, the sights were poorly placed and aligned, and an awkward prone firing position was needed to avoid being hit in the face by the gun's long-recoil action.

A survey ordered by General Pétain in May 1917 shows that many units were only too aware of these shortcomings; however, it also revealed that when the gun worked, it worked well. Citations for medal winners show that the Chauchat could be used as its inventor had envisaged:

Soldat Carpentier, 20e RI, near Nogentel, Oise, 31 August 1918 ... he advanced on the enemy, firing while walking, the rest of the platoon led by Sergeant Berthault. He succeeded in manoeuvring around the flank of an island of resistance and in capturing, with his comrades, four machine guns and twenty-five German gunners.

Carpentier received the Croix de Guerre with palm.

Trench Artillery
The main French field gun, the 75mm 1897, although excellent in open country, had proved itself incapable of destroying well-constructed trenches or barbed wire entanglements. Indeed, the French Army had no modern howitzers

The gun line of the 20e RA, part of the 9th Corps. The 'Seventy-five' was an excellent, accurate field gun, but its trajectory was too flat to make it of much value in engaging an enemy positioned on a reverse slope; nor, later in the war, in destroying wire entanglements. (Ian Sumner)

at all in its inventory; when the need for a weapon of this type became clear, all that was available were 15cm mortars, veterans of the Crimea!

These obsolete weapons were replaced in the trenches by a number of experimental types, including some pneumatic models, but these were all superseded in April 1915 with the introduction of the 58mm Second Pattern mortar, which fired a bomb of around 20kg (44lb), stabilized by fins, to a range of some 1,200m (1,312 yards). Other, heavier, types also saw service, including a monstrous 240mm weapon, but the 58 became the standard. A number of examples of the British Stokes mortar also saw service.

Trench mortars, nicknamed *crapouillots*, from a word meaning 'toad', were served by the artillery, the batteries numbered as 101 to 107 of a number of field artillery regiments. In February 1918, these batteries were amalgamated into five trench artillery regiments (175e–179e). The batteries consisted of 12 tubes each, and they were distributed in such a way that every infantry division could call on the services of a half-battery.

There was one further close-support weapon: the 37mm cannon, based on a naval pattern, and crewed by infantrymen. The first examples reached the front in April 1916. It was an excellent weapon if served well, but its components were too heavy for the crewmen to carry for any distance, which limited its effectiveness. The shield (28kg/62lb) was carried by the sergeant-commander; the tripod (38kg/84lb) by two numbers, and the barrel (48kg/106lb) by the gun layer and the loader. These five men were armed with pistols, while the remainder of the section carried cavalry carbines. Ammunition was carried by other numbers. One former gunner recalled that, in 1917–18, 'our superiors placed us at the end of the column, so we frequently lost touch'.

INTO THE TRENCHES

Early in 1915, Maurice Genevoix, a lieutenant in the 106e RI, observed a column of troops passing through a village. At first he thought they were a working party from a Territorial regiment, but an old friend reveals that they were in fact a new draft from the class of 1914:

The Algerian and Tunisian *tirailleurs* went to war in their light blue uniforms. These were quickly revealed as unsuitable for modern warfare, and so from early 1915 were replaced by khaki, as shown by this Hotchkiss team from the 4e *Tirailleurs algériens*. (Ian Sumner)

They are wearing greatcoats that are too big for them, and slide off their shoulders. They are carrying their packs too high, which chafes the backs of their necks; they rub the area while their eyes stare fixedly ahead, some pale with empty eyes, others red in the face with great beads of sweat, despite the cold. [His friend remarks] 'They're willing, and that will get them so far … but it's not enough, and will soon run out … Too young; far too young.'

New personnel had to adapt quickly when they arrived at their new unit. In his novel *Les Croix de Bois*, Roland Dorgelès, who had served with the 39e RI, describes the arrival of three newcomers:

Observing the effects of machine gun fire in the front line. The shallow nature of the trench suggests that this may be in Flanders. The sides of the trench are revetted with wicker panels. (Ian Sumner)

We were all on our feet, and formed a curious circle around the three bewildered soldiers. They looked at us, and we looked at them, with no one saying anything. They had just come from the rear, they had just come from the cities. Only yesterday, they were walking the streets, looking at women, trams and shops. Only yesterday, they were living like men. And we looked at them amazed, envious, like travellers arriving in a fantasy land.

It required all the leadership skills of squad, platoon and company commanders to blend the new faces into one unit. But it was the squad that would quickly become the soldier's world. There were 16 squads (*escouades*) in each company, organized into four platoons (*sections*). Each squad consisted of 15 riflemen, commanded by a corporal. The new soldier soon learned that his regiment was the best, particularly when compared to other arms of service. Certain regiments had acquired an elite reputation even before the outbreak of the war, each with its own traditions and esprit de corps. The light infantrymen of the *chasseurs à pied*, for example, whose peacetime uniform was dark blue, disdained the colour red as the symbol of 'mere' line infantry; the 'r-word' could only be spoken in three specific connections – the colour of the French flag, the colour of the ribbon of the Légion d'Honneur, and the colour of the lips of one's beloved. Everything else was *bleu-cérise* – 'cherry blue'. The *chasseurs* tried to maintain their distinctive uniform for as long as possible after horizon blue was introduced, simply to emphasize their difference, and thus 'superiority'.

Some units acquired a heroic reputation during the course of the war: the most notable of these was perhaps the *Régiment d'Infanterie Coloniale du Maroc*. Originally created from a number of battalions that happened to be serving in Morocco at the outbreak of the war, it became a formidable regiment, acquiring more citations than any other (indeed, a new distinction, in the form of a double lanyard, had to be invented just for them). Other celebrated formations included the 'Iron Division' of Foch's 20e Corps, the 'Aces Division' (the 14e DI), the Breton regiments of the 10e and 11e Corps, and the northerners of 1er Corps, whose towns and villages were right in the front line.

 D **1918**

The summer of 1918 saw many men abandon their greatcoat in favour of the tunic. This man (**1**) carries the ARS gas mask, introduced in late 1917. Service in the trenches was recognised in 1916 by the award of chevrons, worn on the sleeves. On the left sleeve the first chevron commemorated twelve months' service, and each extra chevron a further six months' front-line duty. Each wound was also marked by a chevron on the right sleeve.

The French made several unsuccessful attempts to reduce casualties from enemy sniping by using visors attached to the front of the helmet. The design shown here (**2**), the third proposed by *Médecin-aide-major* Polack in 1918, was no more successful than its predecessors. Difficult to manufacture, and of questionable value in the field (since the perforations which allowed the wearer to see meant the visor was no longer bulletproof), none were used in anything more than experimental numbers.

The army had always used small marker flags (*fanions*) to mark out ground in camps or for parades. But these were plain, functional items. Carrying regimental colours into the front line was forbidden early in the war, but this meant that there was nowhere to display the awards of the Croix de Guerre. The *fanions* now came into their own and quickly became a feature of parades as far down as company level. The 156e RI (**3**) was garrisoned in Toul, in Lorraine, and their *fanions* bore traditional emblems from that region. The *fanion* of the 11e *Cuirassiers à Pied* (**4**), a cavalry unit converted to infantry in 1916, depicts the dragon slain by St George (the patron saint of cavalry).

2

3

1

4

Hunting for an enemy every bit as persistent as the Germans: a quiet moment allows these men to search their clothing for lice. (Photo RMN Anon)

As the war progressed, squad organization changed, due in part to manpower pressures, and in part to technical innovation like the introduction of the Chauchat automatic rifle and of specialist bombers, armed with either hand grenades or the Vivien-Bessières rifle grenade. In 1916, the fourth company of each battalion was withdrawn to form the divisional depots, and three machine gun companies were created within each regiment. At the same time, changes were made to the platoon organization of the rifle companies, so that one half-platoon consisted of a bombing squad and a Chauchat squad, whilst the second consisted of two squads of riflemen, each with two VBs. The first platoon was commanded by the senior lieutenant, the second platoon by the third senior, the fourth by the second senior, and the third platoon by the adjudant.

Squad organization changed once more in September 1917. Now both half-platoons contained a bombing squad and a Chauchat/VB squad, and this remained the case for the remainder of the war. A further reorganization was introduced in October 1918 – each platoon was now to consist of three combat 'groups' of 13 men, each in turn made up of a Chauchat team and a bombing team – but it was too late to see service.

The machine gunners formed separate companies within the regiment; administratively these were part of regimental headquarters, but in practice one served with each battalion. Like their counterparts in the British Army, French machine gunners saw themselves as an elite. According to Lafond, 'They feel somewhat superior to – or at least different from – the ordinary companies.' Yet their own high opinion of themselves was not always reciprocated by their comrades in the infantry battalion. Machine gunners were frequently dismissed as 'dug-outs' (*embusqués*) – soldiers who served well away from the front line and its dangers. They were excused standing watch, and so generally got a good night's sleep, unlike the ordinary rifleman; and because they were obliged to stay near their weapons at all times they were also excused from working parties. Privileges like these were unlikely to endear them to the ordinary infantryman.

Like many of his comrades, Georges Demonchy, of the 4e *Régiment de Zouaves*, had a finely honed sense of who was, or was not, a dug-out:

Corporals and soldiers were not dug-outs: they manned, and suffered in, the trenches; they occupied advanced posts and went on patrols. But sergeants were dug-outs, as were machine gunners, artillerymen, officers, the regimental transport, and staffs at regimental, brigade and divisional level. In addition, heavy artillery, engineers, aviators, drivers, and all the services at the rear were thought of as dug-outs by the division, and even more so by those at the front.

This seems a little hard on the engineers, at least. All army signallers were part of the 8e *Régiment de Génie*, serving in small detachments along the front, and they suffered many of the same hardships as the infantry. Despite the best efforts of the signallers, communications between units remained difficult because repeated bombardments broke telephone and telegraph wires. This put an extra burden on the company runners, many of whom were killed. Engineers also engaged in mining operations along most of the Western Front, but particularly at the hilltop villages of Les Eparges in the Woëvre, south of Verdun, and at Vauquois in the Argonne. Both villages disappeared in the frequent explosions, and the summit of the crest of Vauquois was reduced in height by 18 metres (20 yards). The field artillery remained unpopular with those in the front line, for many could quote examples of friendly batteries firing too short into their own men, despite the frantic use of signal flares. Trench artillery, on the other hand, was respected for its work in defence, but soldiers knew that if the trench artillery was suddenly reinforced, then an offensive was in the air.

Non-commissioned officers (in the French Army, the term was applied only to those with the rank of sergeant and above; corporals counted as 'Other Ranks') were all promoted private soldiers. The number of NCOs had been severely depleted by the two-year conscription period introduced

The prospect of a hot meal attracts a hungry audience, transcending any language barrier. Cooks were often categorized with the 'dug-outs', since they were always stationed in the rear, perhaps 500–600 metres behind the front line. Nevertheless, they were often the target of enemy bombardments, as the smoke of the cooking fires gave away their positions. (IWM, Q10865)

in 1905. The return to three years did not take place until 1913, and it was only in their third year that prospective NCOs found their feet. The best of the men who looked to the military for a career tended to become officers; and of the remainder, many sought out a comfortable administrative post, with a view to the civil service post that became their due after 15 years' service. Consequently the number of trained NCOs at the outbreak of war was low. Each sergeant commanded a half-platoon of two squads.

Some officers were products of the Academy at St Cyr, but French government policy ensured that perhaps as many as 60 per cent were recruited from the ranks, after a one-year course at the school at St Maixent.

One soldier acts as barber for the rest of the squad. (Photo RMN Anon)

In 1914, applications for St Cyr were falling, following the Dreyfus affair and the official disfavour that subsequently hung over the army; as many as 1,000 posts for lieutenants stood vacant. Most junior officers were drawn from the professional classes – teachers and small businessmen – particularly after mobilization. The casualties inflicted on officers from every regiment during the Battle of the Frontiers meant that their ranks contained a much larger proportion of promoted NCOs than had previously been the case. In November 1914, 15 of the 21 second lieutenants of the 39e RI fell into this category, in addition to three of the company commanders. By 1916, in the 129e RI, only two of the 12 captains, three of the nine lieutenants and two of the 16 second lieutenants had pre-war experience.

At the outbreak of war, a soldier's pay stood at one franc a day. And, during the war, an extra franc a day was paid as a 'trench allowance' (of which half, 50 centimes, was retained as an end-of-service gratuity). But even a packet of tobacco cost 40 centimes, so soldiers had little money to spend. Promotion would certainly mean a pay increase – a sergeant, for example, could earn just over two francs a day in basic pay. Promotion to the rank of corporal or sergeant lay in the hands of the company commander; further progression, to the ranks of *sergent-major*, *adjudant* or *adjudant-chef*, was a decision for the colonel.

Officers messed together, as did the NCOs. Pierre Chaine, who served with three different infantry regiments, noted that 'Officers talk about women, non-coms about pensions and promotion, but the soldiers talk about wine.' And then he added, 'But love is rare, wine dear, and promotion only seldom.' The difference between the ranks was noticeable in other areas as well, with signs that spoke of 'lavatories for the officers, toilets for the NCOs, and latrines for the men'.

OPPOSITE
Snatching a meal in a front line trench. The men wear képis and a mixture of dark blue and horizon blue greatcoats, suggesting a date sometime in 1915. In the trench, only the firestep to the right has any kind of reinforcement. (Photo RMN Henri Terrier)

Food

Two ration scales were in operation, depending on the type of activities currently occupying the regiment. Both included a daily ration of 700g of bread, 600g of fresh meat and 300g of tinned meat, plus 50cl of wine, or 1l of beer or cider, or 6.25cl of spirits. The main difference between the two scales lay largely in the provision of extra potatoes, pasta, sugar and coffee. Tinned sardines in oil were often substituted for the meat portion. In Muslim regiments, rations contained no pork and no alcohol.

Every regiment had a reserve of food, sufficient for several days – tinned, stringy beef in gravy (known sardonically as 'monkey'), a dozen pieces of hardtack per man, packets of sugar, coffee tablets and packets of dried soup – but naturally, the men preferred to eat something fresher if at all possible. A small sum of money, administered by the sergent-major (the NCO in charge of company administration), was available for each company to spend on local produce, where it could be obtained, to supplement the food provided by the army. In some rear areas, cooperative shops were set up, where soldiers could also buy extras for themselves.

> The main meal of the day was supposed to be served at 10am for other ranks, 10.30am for the NCOs, and half an hour later for the officers. The colonel ate at midday, and generals often later than that. But this was not always possible during a relief, or a more permanent move, nor, all too frequently, during attacks: 'We ate whenever we could, in case we couldn't eat when we wanted to.'

The company's mobile cookers were stationed in the second line of trenches, or even further to the rear, and the food had to be carried up to the front line by working parties drawn from each platoon or squad. This was by no means an easy duty to perform. At Verdun, a party from the 18e *Bataillon de Chasseurs à Pied* (BCP) took all night to do so: 'they returned, dropping with

A group of soldiers enjoy a quiet game of cards in a dug-out. (Photo RMN Anon)

A rather more solidly constructed trench, using blocks of local stone, in the Tête de Faux sector (Vosges). The drying washing adds a certain domestic touch. (Photo RMN Emile Le Play)

fatigue, at dawn, the last hundred yards under enemy machine gun fire. Exhausted by the strain, they declared they would rather starve to death than do that again; but in the evening, moved by a sense of duty and comradeship, they set off again across the cratered ground.'

Some men were appreciative of the efforts of the cooks in turning out meals under difficult circumstances; others, like Jacques Meyer, a lieutenant serving with the 329e RI, were less impressed:

> The main meal of the day, called 'soup' no matter what it was, consisted of meat, either with a rubbery lump of pasta or rice, or with beans, more or less cooked, or potatoes, more or less peeled, in a brown liquid, only just distinguishable from a slick of congealing fat that lay over it. There was no question of green vegetables, nor of vitamins …
>
> To wash it down came milky, well-sugared coffee and red wine.

If mud was a major part of soldiers' lives, it was from necessity; wine, however, played a major role from choice. The wine, *pinard*, was simple *vin ordinaire*; nevertheless, it was a true lifter of men's spirits, despite the constant suspicion that it had been watered down by the company cooks. Many battalions in rest areas found a pretext for sending a party to visit a nearby village, complete with 20 or 30 water bottles, to fill up with wine. The canny soldier would have made sure to fire a blank round into his water bottle for just such an occasion; the gases from the discharge expanded its capacity beyond the standard 2 litres. As one trench newspaper put it, 'Water, the ordinary drink of the soldier; wine, the extraordinary drink of the soldier.' Spirits, in the form of an *eau-de-vie* called *gnôle*, were sometimes distributed before an attack or in extremely cold weather, at the rate of one-eighth of a

41

Men take a pause in a Russian sap before going over the top in the Souvain sector. The tension is palpable, but for one man it is already too late. (Photo RMN Anon).

litre for each squad. Since the same ration of wine and spirits was issued to a squad, no matter how many men were present on duty, the true skill of a corporal lay in his ability to divide up the liquid into equal portions.

Throughout the war, many soldiers received parcels, sent either from home or from a penpal. These included knitted gloves and scarves in a variety of surprising colours, food and tobacco. Food was always the most highly prized since for many men it came from their own, or a neighbouring, farm – hams, sausages, pâtés, *rillettes* and *confits*, or cakes. Shared with the rest of the squad, following the unspoken rule, these always provided a welcome supplement to the regulation diet. For men without family, or those from the south and far from home, acquiring a female penpal (*marraine de guerre*) provided a human element, an evocation of peacetime normality, lacking in the front line. Some of these relationships prospered and, at the end of the war, became permanent; but even if that were not the case, a penpal could still be a reliable source of home comforts.

During the day, perhaps one-quarter of the unit was on duty at any one time; at night, one-half spent periods of 2 hours as sentries. Much of a soldier's day (and night) was taken up with working parties. During the day, there were old trenches to repair, new ones to dig, gabions to make and fill, and details to bring up supplies – wire, sandbags, ammunition – from the reserve lines. At night, it was possible to work on the trench defences, repairing the wire and, in the early days of trench warfare at least, clearing long grass from No Man's Land; stretcher-bearers could venture out to retrieve the wounded, and parties went off to bring up food and water.

Many dug-outs, particularly those in the front line, were simply 'funk holes', scraped in one wall of the trench. Philippe Barrès, serving with the dismounted 12e *Régiment de Cuirassiers*, offered this advice to the prospective trench dweller: 'Don't stick your legs outside your scrape, if it's raining; don't lift your eyes up, or the rain will get in them; don't move your arms, or freezing water will run under your blanket … but don't forget to move or you'll freeze. And don't fall asleep.' More permanent dug-outs were constructed, if there was any timber about, with the aid of a tent section to catch the water. In the rocky countryside of the Vosges, soldiers could sleep in small wooden huts they built themselves, placed on the reverse slopes. Soldiers fighting in the chalk hills of the Vauquois, like André Pezard, serving with the 46e RI, may have thought themselves luckier than those further north: 'Along steps that went down 15 metres below ground level were bunk beds which took up half of the passage. It was our dormitory, our living room and our dining hall. Its occupants gained in security what they lacked in ventilation.'

'Torn from his regular job, from his home and his family,' wrote a contributor to the newspaper of the 227e RI in 1915, 'the French citizen is from one day to the next a warrior, ready for anything, or a builder, engineer, bricklayer, marksman, bomber, machine gunner, cook.'

But of all a soldier's skills, the most prized was the ability to sleep. Sentry duty and bombardments quickly disrupted normal sleep patterns; added to this was the fatigue brought on by working parties, so soldiers had to learn to snatch sleep where they could. As one soldier recalled, 'I quickly learned how to sleep in wet boots, because you couldn't get them back on once you'd taken them off, to sleep for four hours in a sodden greatcoat, in the middle of explosions, shouting and foul smells.' Jean-Louis Delvert, in the trenches of Verdun with 101e RI, complained, 'Impossible to have the briefest rest. We are devoured by fleas – when we're not under fire, you can feel them biting. That Saturday, I noted in my diary that I hadn't slept for nearly 72 hours.' Some fleas were so persistent that many French soldiers were convinced they had been decorated with the Iron Cross for their contribution to the German war effort.

Rats were equally disruptive to a good night's sleep, as Jacques Vandebeuque, serving with the 56e BCP in front of Les Eparges, found:

The problem of crossing no-man's land safely exercised many minds throughout the war. These 'Walker Shields' (bouclier Walker) were intended to allow the men inside to cut the enemy wire, although it is difficult to imagine how the occupants could manage to steer and cut wire without exposing themselves to fire. (photo RMN Anon)

Rats, rats in an incalculable number, are the true masters of the position. They multiply in their hundreds in every ruined house, in every dug-out … I've spent some terrible nights: covered by my galoshes and greatcoat, I've felt these awful beasts working on my body. There's fifteen to twenty of them to every one of us, and after eating everything, bread, butter, chocolate, they start on our clothes. Impossible to sleep in these conditions: a hundred times a night, I throw back my blanket and the fright I give them with a light is only temporary. Almost immediately, they're back, in even greater numbers …

IN ACTION

The reality of war came as an enormous shock to the men of 1914. 'We were not paper soldiers,' wrote Jean Galtier-Boissière, a corporal serving with the 31e RI, 'but all most of my comrades knew of war came from patriotic prints.' His comrades were soon to be disillusioned. On 24 August 1914, they were in action. Just as bayonets were fixed, the sun came out to illuminate a 'moving forest of bayonets':

In front of us was a completely empty hillside: not a tree, not a wall, not a fold in the ground … Bullets whistled, shrapnel burst; big shells burst in huge pillars of earth … Deafened, ears ringing, you couldn't hear orders being shouted … Deaf, mute, stupefied with dust and noise, I walked on hypnotised. One single thought, one idea … Forward! Forward!

[The bugler sounds the charge.]

A posed photograph from peacetime. The men are all wearing their packs; the sergeants (kneeling on the right) do not. Note the reserve ammunition pouch, worn in the small of the back. An officer kneels behind. (Ian Sumner)

Now we are moving forward in bounds, following a signal from the adjutant … you run straight ahead, your pack weighing you down, burdened by pouches, water bottle, haversack, which all wrap themselves around your legs … then throw yourself onto the ground … men are tripping over, others are hit in the head as they get up. The bullets arrive in storms, very low down … 'We're being crucified by machine guns,' my neighbour says, before collapsing.

Another bound! … The enemy that is machine-gunning us is still invisible. We haven't even fired a single round yet. There's only about a dozen of us now … I'm huddled behind two piles of earth. Listening to the machine guns clatter: tac-tac-tac. The bullets whistle past: what a hellish din. Every shot I hear, I think, 'This one's mine.'

How long are we there? … Why is no-one giving any orders? And what is our artillery doing?

Suddenly someone shouts, 'Fall back!' Wonderful … The adjutant points us towards a small field of potatoes. On my knees and elbows, I start off, my face nearly on the boots of the man in front. Made it! Bullets are landing all around me, cutting off leaves … we're about twenty metres from a main road with trees running along the side of it … The ditch is safety. But it means crossing an area swept by fire. Tricky moment! One man leaps up, takes a few steps, then collapses, face on the ground … Another goes, and gets halfway before rolling like a shot rabbit, holding his stomach, shouting, 'Oh! Oh!' A third man tries, suddenly stops and turns, his face all bloody, and collapses, crying for his mother … I'm last, I run as fast as I can and throw myself into the bottom of the ditch: safe!

Our losses are very high. The lieutenant-colonel, the battalion commander, and three-quarters of the officers are out of action … Everyone looks downcast, and talks in hushed tones. The regiment appears to be in mourning.

The nature of these early battles was essentially linear, as envisaged by pre-war theorists such as Grandmaison and Foch. Each battalion moved to contact by throwing out skirmishers, whilst holding the remainder of its men in columns in reserve. Each platoon of 50 men was spread out over 100 to 200 metres (109 to 219 yards) of ground, with the men in pairs – far too widely spaced

Another photo from the peacetime manoeuvres. Having imposed their will on the enemy, the men rise and deliver a charge. If this is indeed representative of what took place in 1914, then such a mass of men would have provided an easy target for the enemy, whatever the colour of their uniform. (Ian Sumner)

In September 1914, a new greatcoat – single-breasted and featuring a deeper collar – was designed. However, this was replaced in 1915 by a second pattern, double-breasted with additional pockets in the skirts and a self-belt at the rear. This pattern became the daily uniform of the infantryman, except in the warmest of weather.

A specially lightened attack order was introduced in 1915. The pack was now to be left in the second line; instead, rations and spare ammunition were rolled up in a blanket and worn bandolier-style. Later experience at Verdun showed how difficult it was to keep men in the front line supplied with fresh water, so every man was given a second water bottle.

The principal role of the Chauchat was to provide a mobile barrage during the advance. This required skilled teamwork on the part of the crew, changing the magazines while on the move to keep up the volume of fire. Yet for the individual rifleman, firing during the advance was discouraged, as it was felt that it simply slowed forward progress. Firing, by the platoon or half-platoon, was permitted only to cover its own advance or that of a neighbouring platoon, or to deal with a knot of enemy resistance.

The men of the new fire and support teams were given new equipment for their spare ammunition. The Chauchat gunners each wore semi-circular pouches on the waistbelt, containing one spare magazine each, as well as a pack containing a further eight magazines and 64 loose rounds, and a haversack containing a further four magazines.

The rifle grenadiers and bombers each carried a special haversack, which held the grenades in individual pouches inside. The rifle grenade cup was carried in its own pouch attached to the user's waistbelt.

The P gas masks were superseded in early 1916. The M2, shown here, was introduced later in the same year, and remained in use until 1918.

for effective command. Once contact had been made, troops were fed into the firing line with two objectives – to suppress enemy fire and, with the support of the field artillery, to inflict sufficient casualties to make the opposing line waver. Then, once the enemy lost the desire to continue the firefight, a bayonet charge was supposed to deliver the coup de grace. Victory would result, therefore, not from superior tactics, or even superior weaponry, but from the imposition of superior will. Attacks of this type failed for several reasons: the strength of defensive firepower was underestimated, coordination with the artillery was poor, with assaults frequently launched without waiting for the guns to come up, and the lack of heavy artillery and howitzers meant that the enemy could make themselves safe by taking cover behind any kind of crest.

Although at grass-roots level artillery and infantry tactics were continually evolving during 1915 in response to battlefield experience, the French lacked the material preponderance and tactical sophistication needed to subdue the equally dynamic German defence. Instead of 'fire and movement', with infantrymen covering each other by rifle fire as they moved in alternate groups, the whole line advanced together, keeping as close to the barrage as possible. The enemy, it was hoped, would be so disorientated by the bombardment that the infantry could simply occupy the ground conquered by the artillery. Each failed attack resulted in a bombardment more powerful than its predecessor, yet the artillery barrage remained ineffective. A persistent shortage of heavy artillery forced the army into reliance on a weapon – the 75mm field gun – which was actually incapable of destroying wire entanglements.

The introduction of the Chauchat and the VB rifle grenade in 1916 prompted something of a rethink. Each assault now consisted of a number of waves. A first wave formed by the rifle/bomber half-platoons, accompanied by engineers with wire cutters, was followed by a second wave made up of the bomber/VB half-platoons. A third wave followed 30 metres (33 yards)

behind, again consisting of bombers and riflemen, with the role of clearing the captured trench. And behind them came the remaining two platoons of the company, with the VBs on the flank and in the centre, acting as a reserve.

The role of the first wave was to capture the first line of enemy trenches and then move on, with their main objective to gain ground; the second wave acted as a reserve, and could pass through the first in order to maintain the impetus of the attack. The moppers-up of the third wave took possession of the trench, bombing their way along the traverses, and reducing any strongpoints. Formations for the assault were kept flexible. The first two waves might be in extended order, with four or five paces between each man, but the third and fourth could be in columns of squads, to make it easier to manoeuvre quickly. Yet, all too frequently, the pace and form of attacks were ruled by a rigid timetable that left insufficient discretion to local commanders to exploit success.

Virtually from the onset of trench warfare, French soldiers, in common with those of the other armies on the Western Front, were involved in tactical experimentation and innovation. By 1916, the French Army was moving towards tactical methods that emphasized concentrated firepower and the flexible use of infantry. In 1916–17 Nivelle and Pétain refined this method, attacking limited objectives with the heavy artillery concentrations necessary to ensure success. During the battle of Malmaison, in October 1917, General Franchet d'Esperey, the commander of the Sixth Army, successfully introduced specially trained squads of infantry whose role was to accompany

Filling sandbags at the Place de l'Opéra, a large emplacement in the Souain sector (Champagne). It was the location of a casualty station as well as an engineer dump. (Photo RMN Anon)

PREVIOUS PAGE: A PRESENTATION CEREMONY 1918

In September 1914, the decision was taken to reclothe North African troops in khaki uniforms, largely because khaki cloth was readily available in the UK. Delivery of the new uniforms was slow, and over the winter of 1914–15 various combinations of pre-war uniforms – khaki with dark blue or horizon blue greatcoats – were common.

Colonial troops were supposed to follow metropolitan regiments into horizon blue in December 1914. But, again, deliveries were slow, and the first issues only began in March 1915. But few men had received anything like a complete uniform in the new colour when, that same August, the decision was taken to clothe all Colonial troops in khaki. Although cloth was imported from Britain, the change was still slow. Most North African regiments (left) were wearing khaki by the spring of 1916, but some colonial regiments, like the R.I.C.M. (centre), spent most of the war in horizon blue. Recalling their peacetime uniforms, African regiments were permitted trousers rather fuller in cut than those issued to metropolitan regiments.

In contrast to their men, officers (right) were permitted more latitude in matters of uniform, and the letter of the regulations was stretched to the limit. British styles, including the wearing of Sam Browne-style belts, were popular. This man wears a tunic with an unusually high, upright collar, 'British' flaps on his pockets (i.e. straight-edged rather than scalloped), and bellows pockets in the skirts.

the tanks, in advance of the main infantry assault, and direct them towards their targets. By 1918 the French Army had, like its British ally and German enemy, reached a peak of tactical sophistication.

In a series of instructions in 1918, Pétain sought to achieve greater cooperation between air power, artillery and tanks, all acting in support of the assaulting infantry; measures which bore fruit in the counter-offensives of summer 1918. Drawing on his experience of the battlefield of Verdun, where men frequently lost touch with their command posts, he proposed greater emphasis on marksmanship and self-reliance amongst the infantry – concepts previously absent from French training.

Earlier in the year, the French had still been on the defensive. To reduce casualties from enemy bombardment, Pétain ordered that the front line should be only lightly held, preferring a more flexible defence in depth, featuring strongpoints with overlapping fields of fire. Where the commander followed Pétain's orders – as did General Gouraud, the commander of the Fourth Army during the German offensive of July 1918, Operation *Reims* – attacks failed completely. But by no means all of Pétain's generals agreed with his tactics, emotionally committed to the idea that they would not concede a single metre of French soil. During the German Operation *Blücher* on the Chemin des Dames in April 1918, the regiments of the Sixth Army, now under the command of General Duchêne, were caught by the bombardment, taking heavy casualties, and were forced to give up ground so painfully won during the previous April.

However neat and tidy a diagram might look in the training manuals, an attack was still a frightening and confusing affair. Chevallier's novel *La Peur* records impressions of an assault in 1917:

> We are waiting for Zero Hour, to be crucified, abandoned by God, condemned by Man …
>
> Suddenly, the artillery thunders, obliterates, eviscerates, terrifies. Everything explodes, bursts and shudders. The sky has disappeared. We are in the middle of a monstrous whirlpool; clods of earth rain down, comets meet and shatter, throwing off sparks like a short circuit. We are caught at the end of the world. The earth is a building in flames, and the exits have been bricked up.

'Ready, we're going!'

The men, pasty white, numb, shuffle a bit, checking their bayonets. The NCOs growl out a few words of encouragement. Lieutenant Larcher is in the middle of us all, tense, very conscious of his rank and his position. He climbs onto the firing step, looks at his watch, turns and says, 'Ready, we're going ... Forward!'

The line shudders, and the men hoist themselves up. We repeat the shout 'Forward!' with all our might, like a cry for help. We throw ourselves behind our shout, every man for himself in the attack ...

Men fall, bunch up, split up, disappear in pieces. ... You can hear bullets hit others, hear their strangled cries. Every man for himself. Fear has almost become an asset. A machine gun on the left ... which way now? Forward! That way safety lies. Flat on the ground, flames, rifles, men. 'The Boche! The Boche!' The Germans waving their arms, escape down a communications trench ... Some, mad, fire after them ... 'Damn, I'll get you!'

Set-piece attacks like these were in fact the exception. Much more frequent were patrols and trench raids. The staff were constant in their demands for information, particularly on the comings and goings of the enemy. Prisoners, especially those wearing the tunic that bore their regimental number, or those carrying their personal papers, were what was required. That such actions might bring down retaliatory shelling onto the heads of those who took part was of little account. Parties were normally between four and ten men in strength, accompanied by a corporal or sergeant; on important occasions, an officer might join them. Raiders were always volunteers; in some regiments, they became a semi-permanent sub-unit, a *corps franc*.

Actions of this type were common where there was a 'fire-eating' officer. However, many men took the attitude that they would not engage in combat unless directly ordered to do so, or unless provoked by the enemy.

Burdened with messtins and water bottles, a ration party makes its way back to the front line in the Eparges (Champagne). The trench walls are faced on one side with packing cases and wire, and on the other with brushwood hurdles. (Photo RMN Anon).

A carrying party on Côte 425 (Vosges). Their uniforms indicate that these men are *chasseurs*, but they are carrying bombs for 58mm trench mortars. (Photo RMN Anon).

A Christmas Truce certainly took place in the French lines in 1914, as it did in the British (one account, from the 99e RI in Picardy, suggests that hostilities were unofficially suspended for the whole of the Christmas season, from Christmas Eve to Twelfth Night). It is difficult to establish how typical this was, because many soldiers chose not to reveal such incidents to their superior officers. Paul Rimbault, of the 74e RI, recalled a quiet sector on the Chemin des Dames in July 1917, where the German listening posts were only 8 metres (26 feet) from those of the French, and where 'the Boche, sitting on the parapet, smokes his pipe, while the French soldier writes a letter in the same position'. But this seems to have been an extreme example.

Many men saw the enemy soldier as a fellow sufferer, equally afflicted by poor living conditions and a callous staff, and were unwilling to make life worse for anyone by gratuitously opening hostilities. Certainly when trenches were only around 20 metres (22 yards) apart, artillery fire was just as likely to hit friendly trenches as the enemy, so it was in the interests of everyone to maintain a tacit truce. Attitudes like these were deplored by the High Command, a view echoed by men like Antoine Redier, an officer who served with the 338e RI, before joining the staff of Fourth Army: 'Actually, most of our men, disoriented by the war, do not seem to recognize that the German is their hereditary enemy; they dislike him simply as an opponent, but that is not enough … We must fortify the soldier against this ridiculous idea – that the Germans are just men like us.' In his post-war study of combatants' memoirs, Jean-Norton Cru dismissed Redier as a man ignorant of the opinions of the ordinary soldier, and as one who kept or acquired the prejudices of the rear, and argued that his views did not accurately represent the attitudes prevalent in the front line. Whatever the truth of the matter, Redier, whose home was in Lille and thus under German occupation throughout the war, remained a resolute and vocal German-hater throughout the 1930s.

The men of 1914 had gone to war with enthusiasm, to drive the enemy from France and to liberate Alsace and Lorraine. But that attitude quickly wore off after the Battle of the Frontiers and the failed offensives of 1915. Writing on the second day of the Somme offensive, Second Lieutenant Louis

Mairet thought that the soldier of 1916 was fighting not for Alsace, nor to ruin Germany, nor for his country. He was fighting because he could not do otherwise, with resignation on the one hand, but also with an honesty and pride which helped him acquiesce in the sacrifice he was making. Glory – *la gloire* – much discussed as the motive for fighting (although only in the newspapers) was dismissed. 'Glory,' noted one artillery officer, 'was not as pleased with mud as we were … We did not know her; she did not know us. We asked her for nothing; she promised us nothing.'

The soldier, observed Chaine, goes through several stages at the front. First comes the recruit who has never been under fire, and, prey to his imagination, is beset by nerves. Then, after emerging unscathed from a number of engagements, he loses his fear of combat. He starts to thinks that shells will not touch him and that bullets whistle harmlessly by. After a while, however, he begins to realize that this might simply be a lucky streak that will soon come to an end. He becomes cautious and tries to calculate the risk in everything he is about to do. After that follows the final stage, one of sheer hopelessness, when the soldier resigns himself to certain death. The modern version of courage, Chaine concludes, is not to recoil from an invisible and inevitable death.

Discipline

By no means everyone willingly consented to being placed in uniform, or under discipline. In September 1914, the normal court-martial procedure was suspended and replaced by a system of summary courts-martial, where the sentence would be carried out within 24 hours, without any right of appeal. It was in this fashion that, over a two-day period (17–18 October 1914), Fourth Army was able to condemn 31 men to death for self-inflicted wounds, of whom 13 were actually shot. *Soldat* Bersot of the 60e RI, whose case was

The bane of many a soldier's life – a group of gendarmes pose for the camera. Besides serving as provosts, the gendarmerie also provided escorts for supply columns and for prisoners of war, as well as civilian police for the Military Zone, which extended across all of northern France. (Ian Sumner)

reviewed in 1932, was shot for refusing to obey an order to don trousers soaked in the blood of one of his dead comrades. These summary procedures were abolished and the pre-war system reintroduced in April 1916.

From the autumn of that year, the number of desertions began to grow. The return to a more regular system of courts-martial meant that, rather than face summary execution, those found guilty of desertion were placed in the front line as punishment. Where, wondered those already serving there, were *they* to go as punishment? To the rear? Finding themselves equated with criminals did nothing to help morale, already low after the heroic sacrifices of the battles of Verdun and the Somme. The failure of the Chemin des Dames offensive in April 1917 provoked a paroxysm of indiscipline amongst the unhappy troops.

The mutinies of 1917 were not protests against the war itself, nor against war in general; rather they were protests against the conduct of this particular war, against the way in which the soldiers saw themselves as sacrifices on the altar of futile offensives. The mutinies began not during the Chemin des Dames offensive itself, but during the subsequent succession of consolidation attacks ordered by Pétain upon taking up command; those involved were the units which were moving up to the front, and not those already there. Losses amongst officers and NCOs undoubtedly played their part in this, since they had led to a shortage not only of commanders within each unit, but also of commanders at brigade, division and even corps level – of men of experience and judgement who might have been promoted in the field.

During the course of war, approximately 2,300 men (an estimated figure, since one-fifth of the relevant archive has been destroyed) were sentenced to death, of whom 640 were shot (by comparison, the British executed 306 men, the Germans only 48). Only 27 French soldiers were executed for mutiny, and 60 per cent of all executions actually occurred between 1914 and 1915.

The measures introduced by Pétain when he took command in 1917 – the use of offensives with limited objectives, his compassionate response to the mutinies, the introduction of improvements in living conditions and the reintroduction of leave – undoubtedly helped the army recover its morale; yet while some regiments were able to perform well in 1918, others remained shaky to the end.

OUT OF THE TRENCHES

Casualties

The losses suffered by the French Army were enormous. Of those men serving in 1914, a quarter did not return. By November 1914, the 74e RI had already received 1,175 replacements, out of a complement of 2,700; in the same period, the 129e RI had received 1,345 men – nearly 50 per cent of its effectives – as replacements for casualties incurred during the battles of that summer. In the same division (the 5th, commanded by the 'thruster' General Mangin), these same regiments also suffered heavy losses at Verdun. In a two-day attack on Fort Douaumont on 22–24 May 1916, the 74e lost 1,964 men and the 129e 1,334; the four regiments of the division lost a total of 5,359 men. The fort remained in German hands. The following April, the 146e RI, serving in the Chemin des Dames sector again under General Mangin (by this time an army commander, and nicknamed 'Butcher' by his men), lost 41 officers and 1,900 men in one day. In the same offensive, after only five days of battle, a report from General Headquarters noted that 24 divisions were worn out, and 17 needed to be withdrawn from the front line immediately.

During the course of the conflict, 1,350,000 men of the French Army were killed. A further 3,200,000 were wounded in some way, and about one-third of those would be crippled for life. Men killed in the trenches were frequently buried close at hand because there was simply no opportunity to do anything else. Jacques Arnoux, serving with the 116e RI in the trenches at Perthes-les-Hurlus in September 1915, noticed in the side of the trench fragments of crosses, which bore fragmentary inscriptions: 'Under a scrap of red képi, I read, "Here lie soldiers of the 10e RI. Show respect." Next to it, "Here lie fifteen brave men of the 11e RI. Show respect."'

The men of the regimental band acted as stretcher-bearers in the front line. Battlefield casualties were taken first to collecting points in the front line, and from there were carried to the regimental dressing stations, which normally lay in the reserve trenches. Here the regimental medical officer, assisted by an auxiliary (usually a medical student) and four medical orderlies, performed the first triage. Every division also included eight ambulances (in the French use of the word, a medical unit, and not a vehicle); these acted as back-up to the regimental posts. These units treated everyone who could be dealt with immediately; everyone else who had a chance of recovery was sent to an evacuation hospital.

Evacuation hospitals were located some kilometres behind the front line. Here men were held, either in tents or huts, until they could be evacuated to the rear. A small surgical unit was attached to each. Of the hospitals in the rear, only a relatively small number were under military control; the remainder were run by civilian organizations under army supervision, of which the largest was the *Société de Secours aux Blessés Militaires*.

Unloading an ambulance at a military hospital in or around Perpignan. Note the stretcher on the left, which includes collapsible legs. (Ian Sumner)

The army's medical services were caught unprepared for the large number of casualties, and at first lacked sufficient quantities of even the most basic equipment – for example, sterilizers, large well-lit and heated tents, and vehicles that could accommodate stretchers. It was only with the importation of Ford light lorries that evacuation by motor transport became possible. Trains and canal barges were eventually used, but it was not until 1917–18 that they became truly effective.

Convalescent leave normally lasted 30 days but had to be taken at a pre-designated address. Some men, too far from home to return there easily, stayed instead with their penpal, many of whom were surprised to find that their correspondent spoke with a thick country accent, or was even a black African.

Fifteen days in the trenches were supposed to be followed by eight days in reserve. The relief was always eagerly anticipated, even if it did not always go smoothly. As Louis Mairet, of 127e RI, described:

G A FIELD HOSPITAL 1917

Chaplain (bottom)

The determinedly lay Third Republic allowed no regimental chaplains in its army. In wartime, chaplains were permitted only as part of stretcher-bearer units at divisional or corps level, and there were no distinctions between different faiths. However, since priests were subject to conscription like every other citizen, a large number of priests and rabbis served in the ranks. Under such circumstances, the army permitted them to exercise their calling within their own regiment. For disciplinary purposes, chaplains were responsible to their respective commanding officer; spiritually, they had to turn to the bishop of their home diocese or his equivalent – there was no chaplain-general. Chaplains wore either an army-style uniform in horizon blue, or a cassock. Headgear was either an Adrian helmet with a *Service de Santé* badge, or a beret or *bonnet de police* bearing a captain's insignia.

Nurse, French Red Cross (centre right)

The Committee of the French Red Cross Society provided volunteers who served as nurses and stretcher-bearers attached to existing units; they also provided and staffed mobile surgical units (*groupes auto-chirugicaux* or *autochirs*), as well as staffing hospital barges and soldiers' canteens.

All nurses wore this all-white uniform, with a dark blue cape (white in the colonies) for walking out. The cape bore a badge consisting of a red cross with letters denoting individual organisations – CRF (*Croix Rouge Française*), SBM (*Société de Secours aux Blessés Militaires*), or UFF (*Union des Femmes de France*). For dirty, non-medical work, the white blouse (*bourgeron*) was replaced by a pattern in grey or blue. 71,193 women served as nurses during the war, of whom 375 lost their lives. Male personnel wore an army-style uniform, with a Red Cross brassard on their left arm and Red Cross buttons. (Regimental stretcher-bearers wore their own brassard, which bore instead a diagonal *cross pattée* in arm-of-service colours.) Additionally, many wore a badge on their left sleeve, similar to that worn by nurses on their capes, to emphasise their non-combatant status. Stretcher-bearers were organised into four-man teams, which included a team leader who was distinguished by a red cross on his sleeve. Three teams made up a squad, whose leader wore a yellow cross; and between two and four squads made up a group, whose leader wore a silver cross.

Médecin-major de 2e classe, Service de Santé (centre left)

Army doctors were mainly conscripted medical men, including medical students (who found themselves serving as *médecins auxiliaires*). The medical branch was distinguished by its use of a velvet képi band, rather than plain cloth. Every infantry regiment contained eight medical officers, commanded by a *médecin-chef* (typically a *médecin-major de 1re classe* – the equivalent of a major), 16 orderlies and 64 stretcher-bearers. These men manned dressing stations and regimental aid posts in the front line. Every army corps in 1914 included eight field ambulances, one for each brigade, two with the first-line transport and two more with the reserve transport. Every army contained a further 52 field ambulances.

The path taken by wounded or injured soldiers. The *refuges des blessés*, located in the front line, acted as collecting points and dressing stations. From here, regimental stretcher-bearers took the men to the *postes de secours*, where they were dealt with by the regimental medical staff. Men requiring further attention were evacuated to the divisional or corps field ambulances. The field ambulances triaged the casualties as they came in. At least one field ambulance in every formation was converted into a tented or hutted field hospital to deal with those cases in need of minor medical attention. More serious cases were transported by road to the HOE – officially, a Lines of Communication Hospital (*hôpital d'origine d'étapes*), but commonly referred to as an Evacuation Hospital (*hôpital d'évacuation*). From here, they would be routed by road, rail, or even by canal or river, to a *gare régulatrice* – a railway station from where they would be sent to a hospital elsewhere in France.

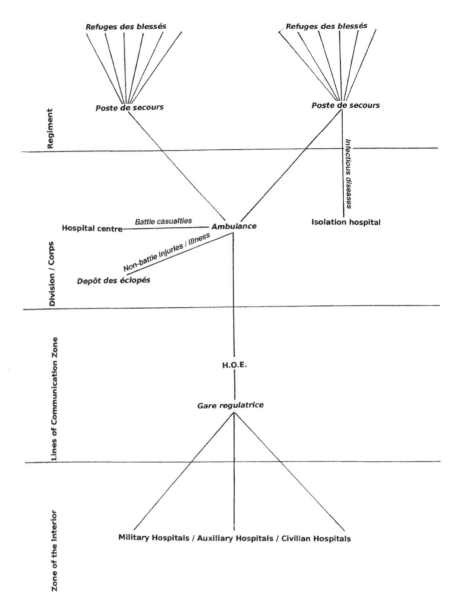

Don't you know it's the relief? We wander around in the night, splashing through the mud. Flares go up, pickets fire; German patrols are out in No Man's Land, their heads are kept well down. The rain is torrential. Finally, the relief begins. Packs on! We set off, stumbling around in the downpour. Squeeze to one side to let a squad pass. Start off again. Arrive at a crossroads, and wait for the 1st Platoon, but they don't arrive. Off again; go to meet the captain on the road. We wait for the captain, packs still on our backs in the rain. He arrives, we set off again, muddy and sodden. Stop at Cauroy. Arrive at Hermonville at two in the morning. Mud, filth. Not a dry stitch on. Tired. Exhausted. We throw ourselves down onto some straw. If you have never done a relief, you will never know what it's like!

'Small' rest periods (*petit repos*) were spent in the reserve front line; longer periods (*grand repos*) were taken further away, a trip by lorry or train. The

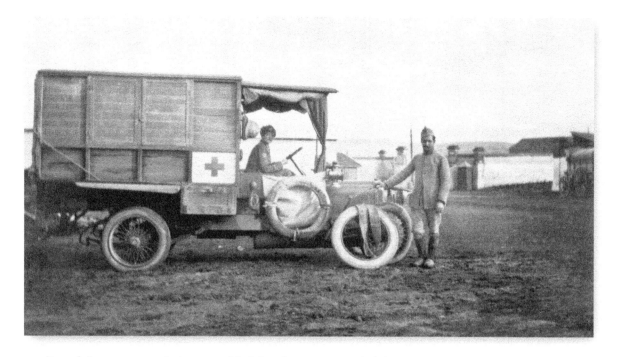

quality of the accommodation provided for the troops varied from sector to sector. In some, the cellars of a village or town provided a safe haven, particularly when the village was far enough away from the front line for many of its inhabitants to have stayed behind. In others, all that could be offered was a pile of flea-infested straw in the corner of a barn. Where no accommodation could be found, engineers were supposed to build barrack huts, but this rarely happened, certainly not before 1917. And rest periods were not always restful. 'Coming from the trenches,' wrote Georges Pineau after the war, 'there were inspections of arms, clothing, boots, hair, feet, field dressings, reserve rations and cartridges; you mounted guards, got vaccinated, scrubbed potatoes, cleaned the huts, washed your clothes, listened to lectures on the machine gun or how to wear a gasmask, took part in parades, reviews and ceremonies with drums a-beating, and, just to keep your hand in, went on exercise.'

Leave was a precious commodity, all the more so because of its rarity. In 1915, men who had served at the front for one year were entitled to a period of six days' leave every four months. But leave, of course, was cancelled on the eve of any major attack; indeed, such was the nature of French strategy in 1915, with attacks taking place all down the line, that leave was unofficially cancelled in its entirety, and was only reinstated when Pétain took charge in 1917. Unfortunately for the man going on leave, his six days began from the time he left his unit and not on arrival at his destination. One real complaint during the mutinies of 1917 was the length of time it took to get anywhere after leaving the front. Restrictions on railway services in wartime were compounded by the layout of the network itself; there were few cross-country trains, and most lines led into Paris and out again. Soldiers from the south or from Corsica might be away from their unit for as long as three weeks. And the problem was actually made worse by Pétain's reforms; once he reintroduced leave, so many trains were going into Paris that the lines became blocked, and men spent hours waiting by the lineside. In response, special leave camps were erected in the Paris suburbs, with accommodation

The widespread introduction of motor ambulances speeded up the evacuation procedure enormously. This particular vehicle, taken at Epernay-sur-Marne, appears to be driven by a British woman driver. (Ian Sumner)

and food. Local politicians were quick to protest about this sudden influx of soldiers, an attitude that did nothing to reassure the men that they were fighting in a just cause.

The sheer number of men called up had also led to manpower problems in civilian life. Over the winter of 1914–15, so many engineering craftsmen had been conscripted that it adversely affected munitions production, and the men had to return to their factories. The shortages also affected agriculture: from 1915 onwards, leave to help with the harvest was given to any conscripted farm worker currently serving at regimental depots, and to anyone serving in a Territorial unit. In 1917, this was extended to include any recently conscripted soldier with an agricultural background.

The gap between the reality of trench life and the way that life was portrayed at home became all too quickly apparent to the ordinary soldier. Paul Boissière, writing for the benefit of his fellows in the trench journal *Le Crapouillot* in 1917, describes a visit to a cinema, where he could not contain his amazement as he watched 'the groups of enthusiastic actors who cross barrages as if they weren't there, and show the credulous how to die with a smile on your lips and your hand on your heart while the orchestra plays a waltz'. Men on leave were asked by curious, but hopelessly naïve, civilians, 'Do you fight when it rains?', or even, 'Do you fight on Sundays?' As men of all nations discovered, their experience of warfare was so different from the life of a civilian that their experiences had to be disguised behind a series of clichés. In 1927, Paul Vaillant-Couturier wrote, 'The divorce between the Front and the Rear did not only stem from the inequality of risk. It was more an expression of the gap between classes – the class of the sacrificed, and those responsible for the prolongation of that sacrifice.'

Not everyone was able to live in the relative luxury of the Villa Monplaisir, opposite, as these two artillerymen demonstrate. For many soldiers, tobacco was one of life's pleasures, and much off-duty time was devoted to carving a pipe. (Ian Sumner)

Sooner or later, every rest period had to come to an end. Paul Tuffrau, an officer of the 246e RI, recorded some impressions of his regiment's departure from the village where it had been stationed:

The Villa Monplaisir, built on a reverse slope somewhere in the Woëvre. Despite its homely nature, the writer of this postcard, a cavalryman serving with the hussars, was looking forward to coming home on leave. (Ian Sumner)

> Men run hither and thither; a quartermaster announces that the coffee is ready and everyone can fill their water bottles; the machine gunners' mules shoot out of a side street ... the young washerwomen of the village, who have been eyeing up the soldiers since they arrived, put down their irons to watch ... this sudden departure to battle; men buckling on their packs whilst holding their rifle between their knees, while they watch and tease them.

Departure often called for some ceremony. Pierre Mac Orlan, a machine gunner with the 226e RI, wrote: 'the company marker flags were uncovered, the drums took the lead, followed by the CO, his runner and the battalion following. One blast on the whistle, the bugles ready themselves with a flourish, and all at once, the regimental march crashes out with all the power of brass and drums. The battalion, in step, arms at the slope, marches off to meet its new fate.'

FURTHER READING

Bach, André, *Fusillés pour l'example* (Paris, 2003)

Brown, Malcolm, *Verdun 1916* (Stroud, 2000)

Clayton, Anthony, *Paths of Glory: the French Army 1914–18* (London, 2003)

Doughty, Robert A., *Pyrrhic Victory: French Strategy and Operations in the Great War* (Cambridge, Mass., 2005)

Ducasse, André, Jacques Meyer & Gabriel Perreux, *Vie et mort des français 1914–18* (Paris, 1962)

Meyer, Jacques, *La vie quotidienne des soldats pendant la Grande Guerre* (Paris, 1966)

INDEX